P9-ELS-000

DATE DUE

COOL CAREERS WITHOUT COLLEGE
FOR PEOPLE WHO LOVE

HOUSES AND APARTMENTS

REBECCA PELOS AND ALICE BECO

Rosen YA™

New York

Published in 2018 by The Rosen Publishing Group, Inc.
29 East 21st Street, New York, NY 10010

First Edition

Library of Congress Cataloging-in-Publication Data

Names: Pelos, Rebecca, author. | Beco, Alice, author.
Title: Cool careers without college for people who love houses and apartments
  / Rebecca Pelos and Alice Beco.
Other titles: Cool careers without college for people who love houses
Description: New York : The Rosen Publishing Group, Inc., 2018. | Series:
  Cool careers without college | Includes bibliographical references and
  index.
Identifiers: LCCN 2016053658 | ISBN 9781508175384 (library bound)
Subjects: LCSH: Home economics—Vocational guidance—Juvenile literature. |
  Dwellings—Maintenance and repair—Vocational guidance—Juvenile
  literature.
Classification: LCC TX164 .B43 2017 | DDC 640.23—dc23
LC record available at https://lccn.loc.gov/2016053658

Manufactured in China

CONTENTS

INTRODUCTION

You might often hear people say things like, "I want my home to reflect my personality," or "My home is my sanctuary." In these modern times, people often work from home, spending the majority of their time in a home office. Some consider their home a getaway from long days of work in an office or other job site. The idea of home has launched networks and TV shows and websites. Small or large, house or apartment, home is important. And chances are, if you're reading this, you agree.

Maybe you're the first to recommend paint colors to a friend who's just moved to a new place. You have an artful eye and a flair for style. You love working outdoors and the idea of planning

Home means something different to everyone. For some, it might be a showplace that represents their personality. Others might think of home as an escape from the day-to-day.

your own schedule. You might be a home enthusiast! And the good news is that home decoration, home maintenance, and the preparing and selling of homes are all viable career paths. Even better, they are careers you can pursue without having to get a college education. All you need is passion, people skills, and a little bit of career building know-how to achieve your goals.

There is a wide variety of careers available for people who love houses and apartments. You can be as creative or non-creative as you feel. You can be good with your hands or a total butterfingers. You can be outgoing or shy. There's a job in houses and apartments for everyone. You might even be able to work from the comfort of your own home! Read on to find out how.

CHAPTER 1

DESIGNER

When you enter a friend's home, how closely do you pay attention to space, lighting, colors, and furnishings, and how they work together to create a beautiful and functional environment? Do you imagine how you could make these spaces more visually appealing? If such a challenge appeals to you, you might want to consider becoming an interior designer.

WHAT THEY DO

Interior designers work with homeowners and other professionals to create design solutions for homes that meet the needs and reflect the lifestyles of their clients. Aside from being creative and artistic, you need to have business skills and be good at communicating and working with others. Most designers are self-employed, while many others work in design firms with several employees. "Large" interior design firms employ anywhere from 50 to 100 designers. Some designers also get jobs with furniture and home furnishing stores and architecture firms.

Interior designers make choices about everything you see in a home. Every color and every wood finish is selected for a specific reason—the ambiance it brings to the room. Interior designers work with clients to make those choices.

Aside from having a background in art and design, interior designers must know how to plan a space and how to present this plan to their clients—both visually (via sketches or computer graphics) and in words. Whereas decorators are involved with decorating the surfaces (walls, ceilings, etc.) of a home's interior, designers deal with the overall design and construction of a house. As an interior designer, you'll need to understand how different materials and products are used and how elements such as color, light, scale, and texture work together to create a specific environment. Designers must know about acoustics (the transmission and echo of sound) as well as ergonomics, which is the science of using information about human beings to design spaces to fit for their needs. A solid understanding of technical concerns, such as the stability of a house's structure, safety procedures, fire safety requirements, and building codes (national, state, and local), is also essential. Knowing where to knock down a wall and what kind of staircase to build are the kinds of questions you must be able to answer.

As a designer, you must be comfortable dealing with people's very different needs and personalities. You must be a good communicator and listener, and be able to understand exactly what your client wants (sometimes he or she might have difficulty expressing his or her desires). Being able to work with others is important since designers often collaborate with architects, builders, engineers, electricians, plumbers, and many other specialists. You must be open to changes demanded by your clients and good at solving problems.

Good management skills are essential since most designers work on tight deadlines and often juggle more than one project at a time. Knowing how to market yourself and your strengths is important since a key part of your job will be presenting and selling your ideas to new clients in ways that are informative and imaginative.

Good interior designers must be organized, especially with time management. Sitting down to respond to a client email is as important as brainstorming color scemes, so you must plan these things carefully.

CAREER PREP

In many states and provinces, you cannot call yourself an interior designer unless you have followed three steps. The first involves acquiring a minimum number of years of education (between two and five) from an institution such as an art or design school or community college whose interior design program is recognized by the Foundation for Interior Design Education Research (FIDER). Subjects studied usually include interior design, art, architecture,

Q & A WITH A PROFESSIONAL DESIGNER

Tina Glavan is an interior designer for the architect William
T. Georgis in New York City:

Q: Is someone born with a designer's "eye" or can it be developed?
A: I feel you're kind of born with it. You can be taught the technicalities, but it's what you do with them that make you a designer.

Q: How did you get started?
A: By chance. I took an interior design class with a friend and
liked it, so I decided to continue and get a second degree. When I
graduated, I got a job through the school's job office and landed in
a prestigious architectural firm.

Q: What are the best and worst parts about your job?
A: The worst are deadlines, long hours, scheduling, delays. The
best? Seeing it all come together at the end and seeing the client's
face for the first time when they walk into their new home.

Q: What is the most important quality for a successful designer?
A: Knowing how to listen to your clients' needs and wants and
being capable of interpreting them into the design of a room or
home.

Q: Did you ever make a really big design mistake? How did you
fix it?
A: Yes. You don't do it again! Basically, you learn from your
mistakes and do it over.

lighting, materials and textiles, business, and marketing. The second step is on-the-job experience with a certified designer or architect, during which time you can build up a portfolio of work. Many young designers start out as assistants to designers or architects—they do project research and draw up design plans. The final step is to pass a certifying exam given by the National Council for Interior Design Qualification (NCIDQ). This is valid in both Canada and the United States. Presently, in twenty-six American states, Washington DC, and Puerto Rico, it is against the law to call yourself an interior designer if you are not certified. After passing this exam, you must follow all the professional standards required by the American Society of Interior Designers (ASID) or the Interior Designers of Canada.

SALARY AND JOB OUTLOOK

A designer's earnings vary depending on many factors. These include number of years of experience and having a good reputation. Another factor is whether you freelance or work for a large design firm with a permanent client list where you earn a regular salary. On average, designers who are just starting out make around $30,000 a year. Designers who are

Whether you learn on the job or take a few design classes in order to learn the design trade, you'll need to be able to market yourself. Building a good social media presence is a great place to start.

also good at managing projects and communicating with clients can make between $50,000 and $100,000 a year.

The demand for designers tends to vary depending on the state of the economy. The US Bureau of Labor Statistics predicts significant growth in jobs for designers over the next few years. However, competition for the best paying jobs will be high. Designers with the most education and strongest business skills as well as talent and determination have the best chance of succeeding.

FOR MORE INFORMATION

ORGANIZATIONS

American Society of Interior Designers (ASID)
National Headquarters
1152 15th Street NW, Suite 910
Washington, DC 20005
(202) 546-3480
Website: http://www.asid.org
This community of designers, industry representatives,
    educators, and design students promotes education,
    events, discussions, and debates related to design.

Foundation for Interior Design Education Research
146 Monroe Center NW, Suite 1318
Grand Rapids, MI 49503-2822
Website: http://www.interior-design.us
FIDER is a nonprofit organization that sets standards
    for interior design courses and certifies academic
    programs that meet those standards throughout
    Canada and the United States.

BOOKS

Artka, Aga, and Jenny Rebholz. *The Brand of You: The
    Ultimate Guide for an Interior Designer's Career Journey.*
    Milwaukee, WI: Henschel Haus Publishing, 2015.

Gates, Erin. *Elements of Style: Designing a Home & a Life.* New York, NY: Simon & Schuster, 2014.

Hale, Robert K., and Thomas L. Williams. *Starting Your Career as an Interior Designer.* New York, NY: Allworth Press, 2016.

O'Shea, Linda, Chris Grimley, and Mimi Love. *The Interior Design Reference & Specification Book: Everything Interior Designers Need to Know Every Day.* Beverly, MA: Rockport Publishers, 2013.

WEBSITES

Because of the changing nature of internet links, Rosen Publishing has developed an online list of websites related to the subject of this book. This site is updated regularly. Please use this link to access the list:

http://www.rosenlinks.com/CCWC/houses

CHAPTER 2

INTERIOR DECORATOR

Teenagers tend to enjoy a space they can call their own. They often do so by putting up art and arranging things in their own manner. Some, however, also want to pick out paint colors, bed linens, and furniture. A few even start giving advice to their parents about the rest of the house. Sound familiar? Are you someone who has always enjoyed decorating or redecorating your room and (if your parents let you) other rooms in your house? Do you like meeting new people and using your creativity? If so, you might want to consider a career as a home decorator.

WHAT THEY DO

Home decorators furnish and accessorize the interiors of people's houses and apartments according to the vision their clients have of their ideal home. Using their own experience, knowledge, and creative flair, decorators help decide what color a room's walls should be painted, what fabrics should be used for a sofa or chair, and what pieces of

As a decorator, one of your first tasks is sitting down with your clients and discussing their wants and needs and how you can create that for them within a set budget.

furniture might look good together and how they should be arranged. Some decorators tackle entire houses while others specialize in specific rooms, such as bathrooms, kitchens, or children's rooms.

As a decorator, you'll begin by meeting and consulting with clients. You'll try to analyze your clients' needs and to determine their budget. Based on this information, you'll develop a proposal that meets the client's preferences and budget. Since you're working with your clients' homes, your main goal is to win their approval of your decorating plans. Aside from acquiring and arranging new furniture, proposals take into consideration space planning or layout, lighting, color schemes, wall coverings and wallpaper, paint, fabrics, flooring, door and window treatments, and use of accessories such as pillows, carpets, plants, and artwork such as paintings and sculptures. Many decorators work directly with new homeowners or with people who want to redecorate an older dwelling. Others, however, work with decorating or design firms or with homebuilders themselves.

Professional decorators need to develop good relationships with suppliers of the products and services they will need. These include manufacturers of furniture, flooring, lighting fixtures, and fabrics (who can give you designer discounts on materials) as well as painters, carpenters, and electricians. Decorators are not only responsible for purchasing furnishings and accessories, but also for overseeing work done by painters, carpenters, and other tradespeople. Often decorators work on more than one project at a time.

CAREER PREP

To become a home decorator, no professional training is required. However, it is useful to have some background in art, as well as math due to the necessity of taking exact

Interior decorators should have a good working knowledge of furniture, including restoration and repairs and spotting a bargain on a quality furniture piece.

measurements and making precise calculations. Since most home decorators are self-employed, some business skills are useful, as are effective communication skills for dealing with clients. However, most important of all is a good eye for design and a strong sense of color.

Most decorators train themselves by taking decorating courses at art schools or community colleges, consulting websites, reading home decorating and architectural magazines, and speaking to furnishings retailers. Visiting design museums and home shows is also helpful. It's a good idea to

STYLE SIBLINGS

David and Frances Adler were siblings who grew up in Milwaukee at the end of the nineteenth century. After finishing high school and university, David studied architecture in Europe and then began designing traditional country homes for wealthy American clients. After Frances obtained her high school diploma, she married a polo player named Felton Elkins and moved to California. When she divorced her husband in 1918, Frances had no means of supporting herself and her young daughter. A stylish and creative woman, her solution was to begin decorating houses for friends. Before long, she was decorating the homes of big Hollywood names such as Edward G. Robinson (a classic film actor known for his gangster roles) and David O'Selznick (the producer of *Gone with the Wind*). Her more reserved brother, David, didn't approve of her flashy clients and extravagant decorative touches. He also thought she bossed around her clients too much—telling them how to set their tables and what kind and color of flowers to buy (pink and red carnations). Nevertheless, he did admire her taste. Together, brother and sister collaborated on many homes and traveled together to Europe to buy furniture. Sadly, only one of their joint projects remains intact today: a house in Lake Forest, Illinois, where Frances lined the library walls entirely in goatskin!

build up your own library of decorating books and magazines for reference. This will help you to familiarize yourself with different styles and stay up to date with new trends. While in high school, ask your parents or friends if you can decorate a room for free. Take photographs of your work (showing rooms before and after) so that you begin creating a portfolio to show future clients.

You can also gain experience and meet potential clients by getting a part-time or full-time job in the industry. Companies that hire interns where you'll be exposed to some aspect of decoration include furniture and housewares manufacturers, retailers (stores selling furniture, antiques, design objects, and home furnishings), and decorating firms.

SALARY AND JOB OUTLOOK

Interior decorators can make anywhere between $25,000 and $50,000 a year. Top-notch decorators with a good reputation, formal training, and a list of wealthy and important clients can make $80,000 a year, or even more. Some of these decorators work for interior design firms or furniture retailers where they are paid high salaries. Others have their own small decorating businesses. However, most decorators are freelancers who often work from their own homes. Clients' smaller budgets and possible gaps between projects mean that freelancers tend to make lower incomes.

At present, the rising demand for professionally designed homes is creating more need for home decorators. The US Department of Labor predicts that jobs for interior decorators could increase by up to 13 percent in the next few years. However, as more people are attracted to design-related careers, there will also be more competition for these new jobs. The more training and experience you have, the better your chances of success in the field.

FOR MORE INFORMATION

ORGANIZATIONS

Canadian Decorators' Association (CDECA)
10 Morrow Avenue, Suite 202
Toronto, ON M6R 2J1
Canada
(866) 878-2155
Website: http://www.cdeca.com
This organization offers information and resources
   for Canada's association of professional decorators
   and designers.

Certified Interior Decorators International (CID)
649 SE Central Parkway
Stuart, FL 34994
(772) 287-1855
Website: http://www.cidinternational.org
This association offers education and certification
   programs for professional decorators.

BOOKS

Henderson, Emily, and Angelin Borsics. *Styled: Secrets for Arranging Rooms, from Tabletops to Bookshelves.* New York, NY: Potter Style, 2015.

Hyde, Wendy. *Decorating for Real Life: The Shabby Nest's Guide to Beautiful, Family-Friendly Spaces.* Springville, UT: Cedar Fort, 2014.

Sikes, Mark D., and Amy Neunsinger. *Beautiful: All-American Decorating and Timeless Style.* New York, NY: Rizzoli Publications, 2016.

PERIODICALS

Architectural Digest
1 World Trade Center
New York, NY 10007
Website: http://www.architecturaldigest.com
This monthly is a vibrant celebration of inspiring decorating ideas, culture, and travel.

WEBSITES

Because of the changing nature of internet links, Rosen Publishing has developed an online list of websites related to the subject of this book. This site is updated regularly. Please use this link to access the list:

http://www.rosenlinks.com/CCWC/houses

PAINTER

Painting can be a satisfying experience that brings some new life and energy to a home. But these days, being a house painter involves more than simply showing up to work with a paintbrush, ladder, and bucket. Using an increasing array of sophisticated tools and techniques, house painters apply paint, stain, varnish, and other finishes to homes in order to protect them and keep them looking attractive. Whether you spend your days outside or inside, painting homes can be an enjoyable way to make a living.

WHAT THEY DO

House painters do more than simply splash paint on walls. They have to know what kind of supplies to select, depending on the surface to be covered. Surfaces can range from stucco walls and parquet floors to a wooden fence or a brick exterior. After taking into consideration a homeowner's preferences, a painter decides what paints or finishes are most attractive and durable and how best to apply them.

House painting often means spending several hours on ladders and on your feet around chemical fumes. It's not a job for everyone, but it can be a rewarding one.

Painters work for contractors, builders, or decorators, or are hired directly by homeowners. Sometimes, they might paint a house that is in the process of being built. Other times, they will repaint a house that is being renovated or restored. Painters begin by measuring surfaces and calculating materials—paint, chemicals, brushes, sponges, tools, etc.—that will be necessary for the job. Based on their calculations of the estimated length of the job and the number of painters required, they present clients with a price for the job.

Painters begin a job by preparing whatever surface is going to be painted. Previous coats of paint or wallpaper need to be removed by stripping, sanding, wire brushing, burning, chemical cleaning, or water blasting. The techniques and equipment used will depend upon the particular surface. Blasting and chemical cleaning are usually for external brick and cement walls. Inside homes, it is necessary to wash all walls and moldings in order to remove dirt, dust, and grease. Cracks and holes should be patched and rough areas must be sanded smooth. Almost all painters will tell you that the secret to a good paint job is starting with a perfectly smooth surface.

A painter chooses to apply paint based on the surface and the effect desired by the client. Some jobs might call for only a sponge or a good bristle brush with a soft edge. Other situations might require a pressure roller or a paint sprayer. Different tools create different textures. Special finishes or sealers provide protection from dirt and moisture.

Working with both paint and wallpaper requires great precision and care as well as good eye-hand coordination. When working on a house with high ceilings or more than one floor, painters need to use a ladder or set up scaffolding—a metal pole structure that includes swing stages. A swing stage is a scaffold suspended by rope or cables that is attached to a roof by large hooks.

As you can imagine, painters need to be agile and have good balance. They also can't be afraid of heights. Being in good shape is essential. Painters need to lift and move heavy furniture and scaffolding. They also spend a lot of time standing, bending, and reaching—repeated movements that put pressure on the back, legs, and arms. Painters use protective gear such as facemasks, gloves, and coveralls to protect them from chemical substances and fumes.

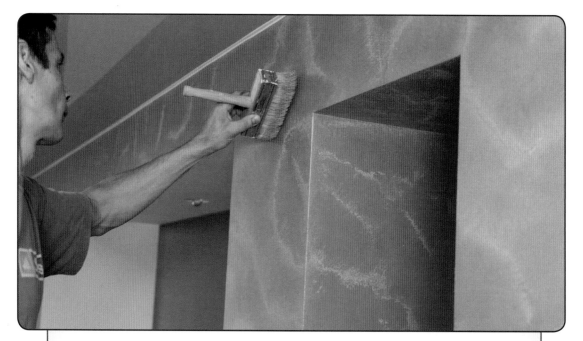

Creative paint application techniques done neatly and well can bring something unique and inexpensive to a room design. You can often find new techniques online or through practice.

CAREER PREP

Most people become house painters after acquiring on-the-job experience. Painting rooms in your house or helping friends paint their family homes is an easy way to get started. Summer jobs with painting companies give you an excellent opportunity to learn the ropes by assisting experienced painters. Many small companies hire students in the summer. Other good places to gain experience are at paint stores or interior decorating firms. In order to mix paints and match tones, it is important to have a good eye and a strong sense of color.

Although not necessary, apprenticeship programs that combine on-the-job internships with classroom instruction can be taken. Common courses include use of tools and equipment, surface preparation, application techniques, paint mixing, wallpaper hanging, and blueprint reading. Apprenticeship programs usually last from two to four years. Candidates must be at least eighteen years old and have the equivalent of a high school diploma.

Experienced painters with strong business skills can become painting supervisors or even open up their own painting firms. Almost half of all painters are self-employed workers with their own businesses, while the other half are employed by painting firms or contracting companies involved in home construction, repair, and renovation.

PAINT TECHNOLOGY

Paints today are produced using sophisticated technology that was developed in the 1940s. However, when it comes to creating special effects, some professional painters discover that the simplest ingredients can yield surprising results. Sometimes, it's just a matter of opening your fridge. Mike Krawiec, who teaches painting techniques in the Chicago Area Painters and Decorators Joint Apprenticeship and Training Committee program, often finishes painted walls by using an inexpensive glaze he makes using a base of flat beer. Another trick is to make a marble-like glaze by mixing color pigment and 7-Up.

SALARY AND JOB OUTLOOK

Painters generally work forty-hour weeks and are usually paid by the hour, although overtime work during evenings and weekends may occur, thereby increasing earnings. In 2015, the average hourly wage for a house painter was around $17.

While the rate of construction of new homes fluctuates depending on the real estate market and the economy, homeowners are increasingly concerned with the renovation and restoration of older houses. Nonetheless, many painters experience periods of unemployment, particularly during

A job done well is the best calling card for a house painter. Often one job will lead to another job...and another!

the winter when painting exteriors is difficult. Since most construction jobs last less than six weeks, life as a painter is rarely dull—you will be constantly traveling to different sites, meeting new clients, and undertaking new projects. The downside to this is that there might be gaps between jobs where you earn no income.

FOR MORE INFORMATION

ORGANIZATIONS

International Union of Painters and Allied Trades (IUPAT)
7234 Parkway Drive
Hanover, MD 21076
(410) 564-5900
Website: https://iupat.org
This labor organization is for painters, paint makers,
    drywall finishers, paperhangers, decorators, and many
    other allied trades.

PERIODICALS

Paint PRO Magazine
Professional Trade Publication
PO Box 25210
Eugene, OR 97402
(877) 935-8906 or (541) 341-3390
Website: http://www.paintpro.net
This print and online trade magazine has tons of
    professional tips and advice for every aspect
    of painting.

BOOKS

Black & Decker. *Here's How Painting.* Minneapolis, MN: Cool Springs Press, 2011.

Sloan, Annie. *Annie Sloan Paints Everything: Step-by-Step Projects for Your Entire Home, from Walls, Floors, and Furniture, to Curtains, Blinds, Pillows, and Shades.* New York, NY: CICO Books, 2016.

Sloan, Annie. *Color Recipes for Painted Furniture and More: 40 Step-by-Step Projects to Transform Your Home.* New York, NY: CICO Books, 2013.

WEBSITES

Because of the changing nature of internet links, Rosen Publishing has developed an online list of websites related to the subject of this book. This site is updated regularly. Please use this link to access the list:

http://www.rosenlinks.com/CCWC/houses

CHAPTER 4

BED-AND-BREAKFAST PROPRIETOR

As the operator of a bed-and-breakfast, you can work at home and live in the house of your dreams! "B&B" proprietors work at creating an original and welcoming atmosphere that allows their guests to feel completely at home. If you like being a host and meeting new people from all over the world, running a B&B could be a perfect job for you.

WHAT THEY DO

A bed-and-breakfast is basically a person's home that operates as a small guesthouse or inn. Visitors often prefer B&Bs to hotels because they are cozier and offer a friendly, home-away-from-home atmosphere. Usually less expensive than big hotels, B&Bs allow guests—particularly those who have come from far away—to come into contact with people from different places.

An important aspect about running a B&B is that you—and your friends, family, or partners, if you choose to

Bed-and-breakfasts are often started in historic homes in communities that thrive on tourism. The Columbia House in Cape May, New Jersey, is known for its Victorian ambiance.

have associates—get to be your own boss. Another benefit is that since you are running your home as a business, many costs—such as electricity, water, heating, telephone, cable TV, decorating, and repairs—count as work expenses and can be deducted as such on your taxes. Depending on how many rooms you choose to rent out, running a B&B can supply you with part-time or full-time income. If your business is seasonal—if you own a beach house that draws in vacationers in the spring, summer, and fall, for instance—you can close down and do what you want with your free time during the off-season. If you prefer to work autonomously as opposed to working for others, this is a great benefit.

To run a successful bed-and-breakfast, you have to communicate well with people and also be fairly knowl-edgeable about houses. Although you can hire professionals such as plumbers and electricians to fix things that go wrong, it helps if you have some background in household maintenance. It is also useful if you can cook well. You have to be attentive to all your guests' needs and maintain a welcoming atmosphere in which everything is clean and

Bed-and-breakfast proprietors handle a multitude of daily tasks. Cooking a meal and planning a menu, often having to keep dietary rescrictions in mind, is just one small part of the routine.

functions perfectly. An eye for detail is essential. Diplomacy and patience are required—not all guests will be pleasant or easy to please.

Although this can mean being on call twenty-four hours a day, much of your work will consist of enjoyable tasks such as preparing meals (most B&Bs include only breakfast), chatting with guests, and helping plan outings and itineraries. However, keep in mind that a B&B is a business. After receiving a license, permit, and insurance, you will need to figure out how to make money. Some questions to consider are: how many guests you will be able to lodge, the price of room and board, any extra services offered (ranging from translation and guided tours to babysitting or pet care), what size staff you might need, and what your reservation policy will be. You'll also need to think about marketing your B&B. This includes advertising at local tourist bureaus, in travel magazines, and through reservation agencies or B&B brokers (companies that will advertise your B&B and take reservations for you). By creating your own website, you can advertise and take reservations on the internet.

CAREER PREP

Starting a B&B requires very little capital (money) or experience and no formal education or training. You might begin by redecorating an extra room in your house or apartment. As long as you're hosting "overnight visitors" on a small scale (one or two guests at a time), you usually don't even need a license.

Most bed-and-breakfast operators learn their skills on the job. To set your B&B apart from the competition, you need to have original services and décor. Courses in hotel management or tourism from a technical school or community college can be useful, but they aren't necessary. Cooking courses will allow you to impress guests with your culinary skills, while language courses could come in handy if you expect to receive foreign visitors. Keeping up to date with travel literature such as guidebooks, travel magazines, and related websites to check out what makes other inns and B&Bs successful is very useful (visiting them

INN SITTERS

What do you do if you're a B&B owner and you want to go on vacation? Get an inn sitter, of course. Inn sitters are substitute innkeepers who take over an inn for a temporary period to make sure everything runs smoothly in the owner's absence. For aspiring B&B owners, this can be an ideal educational experience. At the same time, you can earn income and have the opportunity to travel.

is even better). It is also important to stay attuned to what is going on in the global travel industry. Part-time or summer jobs in the service or travel industry—working in cafés, in restaurants, in hotels, or on cruise ships—can give you valuable experience. Another great way to learn the ropes is by working as an inn sitter.

SALARY AND JOB OUTLOOK

The income of a bed-and-breakfast proprietor depends upon the size of your B&B, the number of rooms you rent, how "full" or "empty" you are, and the prices you charge for the space and services you provide. The more efficient you

You can gain experience in the hospitality industry by working in a hotel or on a cruise ship. Learning quality customer service, especially under pressure, is key.

are at running your B&B—cutting costs while maximizing income—the more money you are likely to make.

The United States receives more revenue from international tourists than any other country in the world. As people travel more and continue to seek increasingly specialized lodgings and services, the hospitality industry will continue to experience new opportunities for growth. B&Bs are ideally suited to the increasing number of

HOSPITALITY INDUSTRY FACTS

- In 2015, the travel and tourism industry in the United States generated nearly $1.6 trillion in economic output.

- One out of eighteen Americans is employed in a travel or tourism-related industry.

- International visitors to the US spent $216.9 billion, and international travel will grow 3.1 percent annually through 2020.

- Accomodations make up nearly 17 percent of total travel and tourism-related spending.

- In 2014, travelers spent around $267 billion on accomodations.

(Note: All statistics are based on 2015 figures.)

budget travelers who have less time to travel but seek a personalized, unique, and homey atmosphere instead of the anonymity of a large hotel chain.

B&B operators have to be sensitive to external changes. For example, in difficult economic times, people have less money to spend on vacations and business trips. Natural and man-made disasters in a specific region can also affect the hotel business. Hurricanes, earthquakes, and other catastrophes can result in cancelled reservations. Criminal activity and fear of violence can also cause travelers to change their plans.

FOR MORE INFORMATION

ORGANIZATIONS

American Hotel & Lodging Institute
800 N. Magnolia Avenue, Suite 300
Orlando, FL 32803
(407) 999-8100
Website: https://www.ahlei.org
This organization offers a large array of educational
   videos, DVDs, books, guides, seminars, and training
   programs that focus on aspects ranging from
   exceptional guest service to bookkeeping.

Professional Association of Innkeepers International
108 South Cleveland Street
Merrill, WI 54452
(715) 257-0128
Website: http://www.paii.com
The PAII provides education, information, networking,
   advocacy, and business opportunities for bed-and-
   breakfast owners.

BOOKS

Fullen, Sharon L. *How to Open a Financially Successful
   Bed & Breakfast or Small Hotel*. Ocala, FL: Atlantic
   Publishing Group, 2016.

Sulich, Susan. *50 Great Bed & Breakfasts and Inns: New England.* Philadelphia, PA: Running Press, 2015.

PERIODICALS

The Bed & Breakfast Journal
214 W. Texas, Suite 400
Midland, TX 79701
Website: http://www.bedbreakfastjournal.com
This is a leading monthly trade magazine for innkeepers.

WEBSITES

Because of the changing nature of internet links, Rosen Publishing has developed an online list of websites related to the subject of this book. This site is updated regularly. Please use this link to access the list:

http://www.rosenlinks.com/CCWC/houses

CHAPTER 5

HOUSEKEEPER

Would you consider yourself to be a tidy person? Believe it or not, people are willing to pay a lot of money to have someone clean up their mess. If you are efficient, good at organizing, and not afraid of a physical workout, working as a housekeeper might be the career you're looking for. In general, you get to work in nice surroundings—the comfort of someone's home—in a situation that is non-stressful. Over time, you might even build up your own cleaning business.

If you enjoy working with people, take pride in cleanliness, and have a good eye for detail, you would probably be a great housekeeper.

WHAT THEY DO

It might seem obvious, but to be a good housekeeper, you need to have good cleaning skills. Housekeepers are familiar with most cleaning products, know how to apply them, and are aware of the surfaces on which they can and can't be used. They must know how to operate equipment such as vacuum cleaners, washing machines, and irons.

Housekeepers need to be physically fit. You'll spend a lot of time on your feet, reaching, bending, and lifting. The ability to take charge and work independently is essential. Often, people in the household you work for may be out all day. Trusting you with their homes, prized possessions, and even pets is a big responsibility. Aside from being dependable, you need to be careful of fragile objects and be attentive to details.

A good housecleaner is friendly, agreeable, discreet, and respectful of the privacy of his or her clients' homes. Some cleaners are lucky to work for people with whom they become quite friendly. If you work for clients that spend a lot of time at home, over time, close relationships can form and you'll find that you have become part of the family environment. This can make your job very agreeable.

Cleaning responsibilities depend on the agreement you work out with your employer—what he or she requires done

Making a bed so that it is neat and tidy and can withstand the tossing and turning of the most restless sleeper without the sheets coming untucked is a skill.

and what tasks you agree to perform. Basic cleaning involves dusting, sweeping, mopping, vacuuming, washing, polishing (furniture, floors, and silverware), doing dishes and laundry, making beds, and tidying up. Sometimes you'll need to use chemical cleansers, bleaches, and other products. Some knowledge of health and safety practices is necessary. If not used carefully, some of these products can be dangerous to you and the environment.

NATURAL SOLUTIONS

Chemical cleansers can be harsh on surfaces, not to mention your skin and respiratory system. Here are some "green" alternatives for common problems:

- For a fresh-smelling refrigerator, place an open box of baking soda or a plate with sliced lemons on a back shelf.
- To leave a room smelling nice, pour some vanilla extract into a cup and let the scent diffuse throughout the room.
- For cleaning mirrors or glass, use a mixture of club soda and white vinegar as the cleaning agent and wipe with newspaper.
- Keep drains from clogging by pouring boiling salted water down the pipes.
- To remove lipstick from fabrics, try rubbing toothpaste on the stains.
- Keep ants out of the house by creating a "barrier" of sprinkled cinnamon or black pepper in front of doorways.
- To polish copper, rub with ketchup and leave the solution on for five minutes before rinsing off with hot water.

Some housekeepers iron clothes, sheets, and table linens; wash windows; and make lunch. You might even walk and feed pets and take care of children. Extra tasks usually lead to extra pay. Work schedules are often negotiated by you and your employers. While some cleaners work in a different house every day, others prefer to work full-time throughout the week at one house (usually a large one). It is up to you to choose what kind of house (a mansion or an apartment) and what kind of family (a single working person or a big family) you would like to work for, based on your personal preferences. Most house-keepers are self-employed workers who work on their own and find their own clients. Others, however, work for commercial cleaning firms that send them out on assign-ments, sometimes in small teams. A few cleaners might actually live in the house where they work, receiving free room and board as part of their payment.

Turnover among cleaners tends to be high. Some cleaners work for short periods in order to earn extra money or to have a second income. Others move on to different types of work or start their own cleaning businesses.

CAREER PREP

No education or training is necessary to be a housekeeper. Most cleaners are simply naturally tidy people with some on-the-job experience. If you get a job cleaning part-time or during the summer for neighbors, this can provide you with experience and some useful letters of reference.

SALARY AND JOB OUTLOOK

The average salary for a typical housekeeper in the United States is around $23,000 a year. Salaries can vary depending on skills, years of experience, and whether you supplement your cleaning with other tasks (cooking, ironing, taking care of pets and/or children). Over time, you might want to open up your own cleaning business. If it grows successfully, you could end up managing a staff of cleaners and earning quite a good living.

According to the US Department of Labor, home cleaning is a rapidly growing field, particularly in big cities. As families with reasonable incomes become more pressed for time, they are increasingly hiring cleaners and cleaning services to perform a growing number of tasks in their houses and apartments. Furthermore, as the North American population continues to age, older people will require cleaners and housekeepers to help them take care of their homes.

FOR MORE INFORMATION

ORGANIZATIONS

Association of Residential Cleaning Services
  International
7870 Olentangy River Road, Suite 301
Columbus, OH 43235
(614) 547-0887
Website: http://arcsi.org
ARCSI and its member companies are dedicated
  to providing consumers a professional and
  quality cleaning experience. ARCSI and its member
  companies are the source of reliable information
  regarding cleaning procedures and techniques.

International Executive Housekeepers
  Association, Inc. (IEHA)
1001 Eastwind Drive, Suite 301
Westerville, OH 43081-3361
(800) 200-6342
Website: https://www.ieha.org
This is a 1,770-plus professional member organization
  for persons employed in facility housekeeping at the
  management level.

Merry Maids
PO Box 751017
Memphis, TN 38175-1017
(800) 798-8000
Website: https://www.merrymaids.com
This company has around 1,300 franchises in the United
States, specializing in finding housekeepers that can
be hired out to work in homes.

BOOKS

Good Housekeeping. *Simple Household Wisdom: 425 Easy Ways to Clean & Organizing Your Home.* New York, NY: Hearst, 2016.
Kondo, Marie. *The Life-Changing Magic of Tidying Up: The Japanese Art of Decluttering and Organizing.* Berkeley, CA: Ten Speed Press, 2014.
MacPherson, Charles. *The Butler Speaks: A Return to Proper Etiquette, Stylish Entertaining, and the Art of Good Housekeeping.* New York, NY: Random House, 2016.

Rapinchuk, Becky. *The Organically Clean Home: 150 Everyday Organic Cleaning Products You Can Make Yourself.* Avon, MA: Adams Media, 2014.

WEBSITES

Because of the changing nature of internet links, Rosen Publishing has developed an online list of websites related to the subject of this book. This site is updated regularly. Please use this link to access this list:

http://www.rosenlinks.com/CCWC/houses

CHAPTER 6

PROFESSIONAL HOME ORGANIZER

Do you ever find that life seems to be getting increasingly hectic? With many adults working longer hours and consuming more, their homes can get quite cluttered. It's hard to get things done, let alone unwind, in a chaotic home. And for the increasing number of people working from home, a messy house can seriously hamper productivity. Instead of drowning in the stress of mess, more and more busy and desperate people are turning to professional organizers, or POs, to organize and simplify their lives. If you're

Everyone needs a little help getting organized sometimes. Big life changes, a busy job, or a move might leave a person feeling disorganized.

a natural-born neat freak, you might want to consider trans-forming your tidiness into a career.

WHAT THEY DO

Being a successful PO involves more than simply getting clients to clean up clutter and throw things away. You'll need to use a combination of experience and sensitivity to design an organizing system that is in sync with each client's personality. Your first step will be an at-home consultation to get to know clients and their homes, and identify goals and problems. In order to break and make organization habits for your clients, you'll have to figure out why a person can't stand throwing out a closet full of never-worn clothes or keeping a room clean. Based on what clients want and how much money they can spend, you can then propose a practical plan of action that will probably involve some of the following:

- Deciding what is unnecessary and getting rid of it (not just throwing it in the garbage, but storing, recycling, selling, or giving it away).
- Reorganizing and rearranging objects and furniture for more space.
- Creating/acquiring storage solutions—ranging from shelving units and cupboards to baskets, containers, filing systems, and bulletin boards.

Q&A WITH A PROFESSIONAL ORGANIZER

Hellen Buttigieg is a professional organizer, a life coach, the TV host of *Neat*, and the founder of We Organize U in Oakville, Canada:

Q: How did you decide to become/get started as a professional organizer?

A: When I saw an article in a local newspaper about someone who organizes homes for a living, I instantly knew it was for me. I joined Professional Organizers in Canada (POC) and signed up to be on the board at the first meeting I attended.

Q: Have you always been a neat/organized person yourself? What was your room like when you were growing up?

A: Although not all professional organizers were neat as kids, I was always highly organized, with strong time-management skills. My parents never had to ask me to clean my room! I realized from a young age that I felt better in a tidy room and I could get more accomplished if my space was organized. Not only was my room always tidy, every drawer had clothes neatly folded and every paper was filed alphabetically. I took great pride in creating a cool-looking room. In fact, I would clip pictures from magazines and then decorate my room to reflect that look.

Q: How do you find clients and keep yourself busy enough to make a living?

A: Most of my clients now see me on the show *Neat* and contact me by phone or email. Before I had the TV show, I attracted clients through my website, by being listed on several online directories, and by conducting organizing seminars for various groups. It takes time to build a clientele and begin to make a living, but if you want it badly enough and believe in your business, it can be done. Overcoming the fear of putting yourself out there is the hardest part.

Q: What's the most extreme clutter situation you've ever encountered?

A: I see extreme clutter situations quite a bit. The most extreme was a large family home where I had to clear clutter just to get into the front door and up the staircase; it was a safety hazard to live there.

Q: What's the hardest part of your job?

A: It can be draining, both physically and emotionally, so it's crucial that I make self-care a priority in order to be fully present for my clients.

Q: What's the most rewarding part?

A: The most rewarding part of my job is having the opportunity to inspire, motivate, and give people the tools to help themselves change their lives. Practically overnight, I see people move from feeling overwhelmed and hopeless to feeling confident and in control of their lives. It's also very fulfilling to use my natural talents and abilities to make a living.

- Redecorating. Different colors, furniture, lighting, and décor can make an enormous difference, creating a more attractive, comfortable and efficient space.
- Creating a list of new organizational routines and habits to prevent clutter and mess from returning.

Although you need little or no money to start up your own PO business, you will need to have some basic business skills in order to control costs and create a successful marketing plan. You'll also need to be aware of the latest organizing trends and products available on the market.

Although many professional organizers work strictly as consultants, others give workshops or write books, articles, and newsletters about organizing. Some also create and/ or sell organizational products. Some residential POs even specialize in certain services and solutions, such as organizing home offices, libraries, closets, kids' rooms, kitchens, and garages. Others specialize in certain types of clients, such as seniors or people with disabilities.

CAREER PREP

Although there are no official manuals or educational programs for becoming an organizer, there are many useful books and websites written by experienced POs. The

A good professional organizer can take a look at a space and begin to make a plan on how to not only organize it but keep it organized.

National Association of Professional Organizers (NAPO) can put you in touch with practicing POs near you who can mentor or coach you. Many POs offer workshops and classes at community colleges, as well as adult education classes. Sometimes, you can work with them as an apprentice or assistant to get on-the-job experience. NAPO provides a certification program that includes specific educational standards and offerings for professional organizers. Check its website for more details.

SALARY AND JOB OUTLOOK

How much you earn depends on how much business you can drum up. Professional organizers who are starting out can earn anywhere between $35 and $50 an hour. Some POs prefer to charge a flat fee for each project. There is usually a difference in whether you are simply consulting with clients or doing hands-on organizing work yourself. If you branch out into giving seminars and workshops and writing self-help books, you can supplement your income.

Professional organizing is an expanding field as people become busier and POs become increasingly specialized (POs who specialize in children's rooms or home offices, for example). Although the competition is growing—thanks, in part, to the popularity of makeover TV shows—smart and ambitious people who know how to design and sell their own unique services can make a good living as organizers.

FOR MORE INFORMATION

ORGANIZATIONS

Julie Morgenstern's Professional Organizers
850 7th Avenue, Suite 901
New York, NY 10019
(212) 586-8084
Website: http://www.juliemorgenstern.com
Organizing expert Julie Morgenstern's work has been
featured on *Oprah*, the *Today Show*, and in the *New
York Times*. Her website offers tips, products, idea
exchanges, and photos of before and afters, as
well as information about workshops and getting
started as a PO.

National Association of Professional Organizers
1120 Route 73, Suite 200
Mount Laurel, NJ 08054
(856) 380-6828
Website: http://www.napo.net
NAPO is North America's leading PO association, with
information and research about every aspect of
this growing industry. Members include organizers,
speakers, trainers, and authors.

BOOKS

Merrill, Douglas, and James A. Martin. *Getting Organized in the Google Era: How to Stay Efficient, Productive (and Sane) in an Information-Saturated World.* New York, NY: Crown, 2011.

Noble, Dawn. *How to Start a Home-Based Professional Organizing Business.* Guilford, CT: The Globe Pequot Press, 2011.

Rayburn, Dana. *Organized for Life! Your Ultimate Step-by-Step Guide for Getting Organized So You Stay Organized.* Medford, OR: Effortless Living, 2013.

WEBSITES

Because of the changing nature of internet links, Rosen Publishing has developed an online list of websites related to the subject of this book. This site is updated regularly. Please use this link to access the list:

http://www.rosenlinks.com/CCWC/houses

CHAPTER 7

HOUSE INSPECTOR

Do you like detective work? Being a home inspector is kind of like being a detective. Using acquired knowledge about building structures, you get to snoop through other people's homes—but for a good cause: to make sure they are safe and in good condition. By examining every part of a home, a home inspector can discover flaws and potential problems and warn interested buyers about these defects. This can lead to a significant reduction in the price of a house. It can also ensure that dreams of home ownership don't turn into nightmares.

Home inspectors visit homes (often in the process of the home being sold) and look for building flaws, pests, and any damage to the home.

WHAT THEY DO

Home inspection is a fairly new profession. Originally, many people shopping for a home relied on builder and architect friends to provide them with knowledgeable opinions about the condition of a house. However, in the 1970s, buyers increasingly began turning to specialists who were trained to look at much more than major structural problems, such as leaking pipes and sinking foundations. Such experts became known as home inspectors. They were hired to comb a house from top to bottom, checking everything from plumbing, electrical wiring, roofing, and ventilation to major kitchen appliances and heating and cooling systems.

As an inspector, you must be able to identify current flaws and predict future concerns. Your subsequent report will include the estimated cost of fixing these problems so that the buyer will know how much he or she will need to invest in repairs. Sometimes the seller of a house will hire a home inspector to identify defects. If they are repaired before the seller puts a house on the market, a higher asking price can be set.

To carry out an inspection, you must have sound knowledge of home construction and engineering. You'll also need to be physically fit. On a daily basis, you'll be climbing up on roofs, exploring basements, and inspecting attics. No wonder some inspectors joke that their best friend is the folding ladder. Other "friendly" tools include electric outlet testers and moisture meters that identify leaks and seepage.

Tasks such as climbing on roofs and checking electrical wiring obviously present some dangers. Most inspectors rarely escape from getting the odd electrical shock or being singed from the flames of a furnace. When crawling through attics and basements, it is not uncommon to encounter dirt and grime, broken glass, bugs, rodents (living and dead), and other unpleasant surprises.

Other risks are of a legal nature. Sometimes, even the most careful inspection fails to identify a major defect. Some problems—such as leaks that only occur when the wind blows a heavy rain at a certain angle—are almost impossible

A home inspector must do a thorough job to ensure that a home is safe and to expose any hidden flaws.

to foresee during an inspection. When such problems show up after the house has been purchased, new owners may feel cheated and angry even though an inspection is not a guarantee. Some owners might even consider lawsuits against inspectors. For this reason, many home inspectors take out liability insurance to protect themselves from expensive legal battles. The threat of such legal risks also explains why most inspectors work as independent contractors. Inspection firms are cautious about hiring permanent workers and having to carry the blame for their oversights. In an attempt to protect themselves, they tend to subcontract inspection work on an individual basis. Nonetheless, running your own inspection business is easy in that little start-up money or equipment is required and you get to be your own boss.

Since you will need to drum up your own business, good people skills are essential. Home inspectors are usually recommended to buyers by real estate agents, homebuilders, and architects. Buyers often accompany you on an inspection, which usually takes between two and three hours. During this time, you will need to outline the home's features in order to educate buyers about the condition of the home.

Following the inspection, you will need to write up a detailed report that will help buyers decide whether to go ahead with the purchase, renegotiate the price of a house, or back out of a bad deal. Although official report forms are available, the ability to write clearly and concisely is important. It is considered unethical to discuss your observations with sellers or real estate agents.

CAREER PREP

There are no official requirements or education necessary to become a professional home inspector. However, high school science courses can be useful in order to understand electrical, heating, and cooling systems. Math is important for calculations, and English composition for writing reports.

Working part-time during the summer for a company that specializes in the construction or renovation of houses can provide you with valuable on-the-job experience in terms of understanding structural and technical aspects of home construction. Other useful jobs include working for an architecture or engineering firm or for an electrician or plumber. Getting an internship (paid or unpaid) at a home inspection company where you can observe an inspector at work is an ideal kind of apprenticeship. Increasingly, technical schools, community colleges, and some online courses are available in home inspection.

Home inspection is not a regulated profession, which means that inspectors don't have to pass any tests or acquire certification. Nonetheless, in light of the serious consequences

of a poor inspection and the competitiveness of the field, increasing numbers of inspectors certify themselves from home inspection associations. These associations—such as the National Association of Certified Home Inspectors (NACHI) and the American Society of Home Inspectors (ASHI)—offer part-time courses and workshops that deal with all aspects of inspection. After gaining some on-the-job experience and passing exams, successful candidates are recognized as certified professionals.

SALARY AND JOB OUTLOOK

Home inspection can be uncertain in terms of steady work. When the housing market is booming, inspectors may carry out three to four inspections a day during a six-day week. However, in slow seasons, competition increases and work can diminish by 50 percent. Most inspectors charge by the job, with fees based on the selling price of the house and its square footage. Despite regional differences, an average inspector in North America earns between $250 and $350 per inspection. Certified professionals with more experience who offer additional services—for example, inspections of swimming pools, wells, and septic systems, and testing for radon, asbestos, lead paint fumes, and termites—can compete for more jobs and earn more money.

rking in construction can provide good experience for a future home
ector. Someone who has worked hands-on with building materials can spot a
orly done job or damage to a structure.

Although some inspectors make around $20,000 a year, others can make up to $80,000.

The ASHI estimates that 77 percent of homes sold in the United States and Canada are inspected before they are purchased. This means that there is still opportunity for considerable growth in the field. Furthermore, home inspectors interested in branching out can expand their expertise to include inspections of commercial buildings. Some inspectors also offer their services as expert witnesses who give testimony in court cases.

FOR MORE INFORMATION

ORGANIZATIONS

American Society of Home Inspectors (ASHI)
932 Lee Street, Suite 101
Des Plaines, IL 60016
(847) 759-2820
Website: http://www.ashi.org
This association for homebuyers and sellers, real estate
agents, and home inspectors is a good source of
information about education, inspection standards,
and job opportunities. Its website includes a virtual
home inspection tour and an online store that sells
inspection tools.

Association of Construction Inspectors
PO Box 879
Palm Springs, CA 92263
(877) 743-6806
Website: http://www.aci-assoc.org
This is North America's largest professional organization
for people involved in construction inspection
and construction management. The site includes
information about professional standards, inspection
guidelines, and training and jobs.

Canadian Association of Home Inspectors (CAHI)
PO Box 76065
Ottawa, ON K2W 0E1
Canada
(888) 748-2244 or (613) 475-5699
Website: http://www.cahi.ca
The "voice" of Canada's home inspection industry, this
    national association offers information on standards
    and a nationwide list of inspectors.

Home Inspection Institute of America
314 Main Street
Yalesville, CT 06492
(203) 284-0288
Website: https://www.nachi.org/hiia.htm
This home inspection association offers training and
    certification programs for home inspectors in the
    United States and Canada.

BOOKS

Conway, Wally. *Home Inspection Secrets of a Happy Home
    Inspector: A Guide to Peace of Mind for Home Buyers,*

Sellers, and the Agents Who Love Them! Chattanooga, TN: Someday Press, 2013.

Holmes, Mike. *Holmes Inspection: The Essential Guide for Every Homeowner, Buyer and Seller.* New York, NY: Liberty Street, 2012.

Mometrix Test Preparation. *Home Inspector Exam Secrets Study Guide.* Beaumont, TX: Mometrix, 2013.

Robinson, Roger C. *The Complete Guide to Home Inspection.* Newtown, CT: Taunton Press, 2015.

WEBSITES

Because of the changing nature of internet links, Rosen Publishing has developed an online list of websites related to the subject of this book. This site is updated regularly. Please use this link to access the list:

http://www.rosenlinks.com/CCWC/houses

CHAPTER 8

REALTOR

Realtors or real estate agents thrive on finding the perfect home for people seeking to rent or purchase an apartment, house, or vacation property. If you love houses, enjoy meeting new people, and have a knack for selling, you will likely take to the dynamic field of real estate.

WHAT THEY DO

For many people, buying or selling a home is one of life's biggest decisions. Finding the right property, negotiating a fair price, finding financing, and closing the deal while respecting local and state or

A realtor acts as an intermediary between someone selling a home and a person (or people) buying the home.

provincial property laws can be an overwhelming challenge. For this reason, most people turn to real estate agents and brokers for help.

As a real estate agent, you basically have to know everything about the housing market in your community or town. This means keeping up with the market value of all types of properties as well as local zoning and tax laws. You'll need to be aware of interest rates—high interest rates make it more difficult to get loans from banks—and learn where clients can seek financing. You also have to be knowledgeable about your community or town. Clients with small children, for example, will probably want a home in a low-crime neighborhood that is close to good schools and recreational facilities such as

Real estate agents work with clients to find out their expectations and try to work within those expectations. A good relationship with clients is key!

parks or swimming pools. Elderly clients, however, might be more interested in quiet neighborhoods with plenty of nearby conveniences. Working with all sorts of different people and trying to meet their needs means you have to be trustworthy, attentive to detail, and a good listener.

More than half of real estate agents are independent workers. They are contracted by a licensed real estate broker—either a small firm or a franchise of a large national company such as Century 21 or Royal LePage. In return for finding properties to sell and then closing the deal between sellers and buyers, the broker pays the agent a portion of the commission earned from the sale of the property. Brokers manage real estate offices, advertise properties, supervise real estate agents, and handle business and administrative details, as well as all paperwork. In the meantime, agents track down new properties whose owners will agree to list these homes for sale with the firm and locate potential buyers. Before showing homes to buyers, agents meet with their clients to get a sense of what they're looking for and how much they can spend. If the buyer likes a certain home but can't afford it, the agent will help negotiate a good price with the seller as well as help find financing with banks or mortgage companies.

As an agent, you will supervise the writing and signing of the contract. It is your responsibility to make sure both parties respect the terms of the contract. For instance, if the seller agrees to make repairs, the agent or broker must make sure that they are actually carried out.

CAREER PREP

You can't work as a real estate agent unless you have a license. For this, you need to be eighteen years old, have a high school diploma, and pass a written exam that tests your knowledge about real estate and property laws. Many licensing associations also require you to complete between thirty and ninety hours of classroom instruction. Local associations that are members of the National Association of Realtors sponsor introductory real estate courses that cover everything from selling techniques to legal concerns.

Many community colleges and junior colleges offer courses in real estate, as well as finance, marketing, statistics, and law—all of which will be very helpful. Real estate firms usually offer training programs and courses for beginners. Generally, the larger the firm, the more thorough the training program.

Getting a summer job or internship with a real estate firm, where you'll be working as an assistant to agents or brokers, is the best way to learn about real estate and make contacts. Starting out in the world of real estate is fairly easy. However, becoming a successful agent who makes many sales and high commissions depends on talent, determination, organizational skills, and having an outgoing personality.

SALARY AND JOB OUTLOOK

Fixed salaries for real estate agents are low or nonexistent. The main source of income for both real estate agents and brokers is the commission that they make on sales. Commissions are a percentage rate of the overall price paid for the home. The rate varies according to the type of property, its value, and what the agent and broker agreed upon. Often commissions are divided between several agents and brokers. The broker or agent that obtained the listing usually splits the commission with the agent that made the sale. The real estate firm that employs them also receives a share, usually about half of the total commission.

As a new agent, it may take weeks or months before you make your first sale. However, with more experience and clients, you can begin making some serious money. Most salaried real estate agents make between $20,000 and $53,000 a year, including commissions. The top 10 percent make over $80,000. The challenge of making good money can be a strong motivating force for many real estate agents.

Job opportunities for real estate agents are expected to grow slowly over the next decade. In large part, this is due to technological advances. For example, buyers can bypass certain steps by simply checking out properties and prices on the internet. Using a computer, an agent can, initially, show clients all of a home's features without having to leave the office. The widespread use of cell phones with internet access has made it easier for agents to share and trade information with buyers, sellers, lawyers, and contractors much more efficiently. Less time is spent driving around from house to house. In fact, many agents don't even need to work at an office but can work comfortably out of their own homes. With individual agents able to take on a larger number of clients, competition is tougher for newcomers.

However, in some instances, buyers depend increasingly on agents—to handle complex transactions such as the closing of the actual sale, for example. Furthermore, as North Americans continue to view real estate as a secure investment, there will undoubtedly be an increase in property purchases, particularly in cities and in new suburban areas.

FOR MORE INFORMATION

ORGANIZATIONS

Dearborn Real Estate Education
332 Front Street, Suite 500
La Crosse, WI 54601
(800) 972-2220
Website: http://www.dearborn.com/recampus/
   reechome.asp
This is the nation's top provider of real estate
   education. It publishes training materials, available
   in print, via software, and online.

National Association of Realtors
430 North Michigan Avenue
Chicago, IL 60611-4087
(800) 874-6500
Website: http://www.realtor.org
The United States' leading organization for realtors
   offers a wealth of information concerning every
   aspect of worldwide real estate. Its website includes
   news reports, industry research, and information
   about education and events.

BOOKS

Yoegel, John A. *Real Estate License Exams for Dummies.*
   Hoboken, NJ: For Dummies, 2013.

Zeller, Dirk. *Success as a Real Estate Agent for Dummies.* Hoboken, NJ: For Dummies, 2013.

PERIODICALS

Realtor Magazine
National Association of Realtors
430 North Michigan Avenue
Chicago, IL 60611-4087
Website: http://www.realtor.org
This print and online magazine is from North America's leading real estate association. It includes articles, interviews, business tips, and selling techniques. The online version features exclusive reviews, columns, and resources.

WEBSITES

Because of the changing nature of internet links, Rosen Publishing has developed an online list of websites related to the subject of this book. This site is updated regularly. Please use this link to access the list:

http://www.rosenlinks.com/CCWC/houses

CHAPTER 9

EXTERMINATOR AND PEST CONTROLLER

Think back to last summer's backyard barbecue. Remember how, aside from your friends and family, there were also a lot of annoying bugs present? Well, other North Americans are equally irritated by these and other bothersome, destructive, and sometimes even dangerous pests. This makes getting rid of them not only a pleasure but also a growing career opportunity.

WHAT THEY DO

Pests are more than just annoying. They sting and bite, spread diseases, and can damage and destroy furniture and homes.

Because they work around chemicals and in homes that have been invaded by pests, pest control workers must protect themselves with the right clothing.

Cockroaches, rats, mice, termites, fleas, ants, bees, wasps, and bedbugs are all common pests that infest North American homes, regardless of whether they are tiny rural cabins or elegant urban penthouses. To get rid of these pests, home-owners are giving up on the cheap, but often ineffective, remedies sold at hardware stores and pharmacies. Instead, they rely increasingly on the services of a pest controller.

As a pest controller, you must know how to locate and identify pests before destroying them. To do this, you'll need to know about pests' habitats and habits. You'll also have to be familiar with the various types of pest management techniques. Applying chemical pesticides is the most popular way of getting rid of pests. "Common use" pesticides—available

TERMITE CONTROL

The most destructive insect in North America is the subterranean termite. These tiny devourers of anything made of wood do more damage to homes than fires and storms combined! If not eliminated, these termites can eat away a house's frame, causing it to collapse. Despite improved technology, every year termites do more than $2.5 billion in damage in the United States alone.

to the public in weak concentrations—are the most widely used. If the pest problem is severe, however, you might need to use "restricted use" pesticides. Potentially harmful to pest controllers, clients, and the environment, such pesticides are controlled by the Environmental Protection Agency (EPA). As a pest controller, you must be cautious when dealing with any kind of chemical. Before you can begin working in this profession, you must undergo training in health and safety procedures.

Other common pest management techniques include setting traps and operating equipment capable of freezing, burning, or electrocuting pests. In some cases, you might need to construct a physical barrier that prevents pests from entering a home or that cuts them off from food supplies. Another common method is to use poisonous baits that destroy the pests or prevent them from reproducing. Increasingly, pest controllers use a variety of these techniques instead of pesticides. Aside from environmental risks, many pests are becoming more resistant to some pesticides.

In general, there are three levels of pest control management, which differ based on training and responsibilities: technicians, applicators, and supervisors (although the names vary depending on your state or province). Pest control technicians locate pests and operate traps. They assist applicators by preparing equipment and dealing with customers. They can apply pesticides only when supervised by an applicator.

Applicators, or exterminators, do the same job as technicians. In addition, however, they are certified by professional associations to use all kinds of pesticides without supervision. Some applicators might specialize in a particular type of pest or service. Termite exterminators often drill holes into homes to get to termites buried deep within wood. To prevent them from reappearing, they might create obstacles by digging holes or trenches around houses. Fumigators control pests by using poisonous gases called fumigants. Before a home is fumigated, it must be completely sealed and evacuated. Other specialties include rodent control and tree and lawn control. No matter what your specialty, you need to be in good physical shape to deal with the bending, crawling, lifting, and other activities that are required by the job.

Pest control supervisors or operators supervise technicians and applicators. Often, they manage or own the pest control firm. They make sure that their workers follow rules and procedures while they deal with the business aspects of the company.

Most pest controllers work standard full-time hours, although many also work weekends and evenings. Since pests thrive in warm climates, there are more job opportunities in southern states where summer months are longer and warmer. In fact, close to half of all American pest controllers work in California, Florida, Georgia, North Carolina, Tennessee, and Texas. The downside to working in warm

PESTS ON DISPLAY

Michael Bohdan has been a professional pest controller for over twenty years. In his hometown of Plano, Texas, he runs the Pest Shop, a store that sells a wide variety of pest control products. He is also the founder of one of the most obscure museums in North America: the Cockroach Hall of Fame. Located in a corner of Bohdan's store, the hall of fame features dead roaches dressed up (in bug-sized clothes) as famous celebrities, such as "Liberoachi" and "David Letteroach." Bohdan also displays three-to-four-inch-long (eight to ten centimeters) Madagascar hissing cockroaches. Not only are these pests very much alive, but they actually hiss at visitors!

weather is that it can get very hot beneath your heavy gloves, protective suits, and goggles.

CAREER PREP

In general, all that is required to be a pest controller is a high school diploma. Aside from good interpersonal skills, it is also useful if you have a driver's license.

Since this job deals with dangerous chemicals, pest controllers have to be aware of many federal, state, and provincial environmental regulations. In many states and provinces, you can only become a certified pest controller by acquiring job experience and passing an exam. In most cases, the best way to begin is by getting a job at a pest control firm as an apprentice technician. You'll receive on-the-job training and take courses that help you prepare for certification as a technician. To be certified as an applicator or a supervisor requires further training and more job experience.

SALARY AND JOB OUTLOOK

The average hourly wage for a full-time pest control worker in 2015 was $15.46. Most workers make between $10 and $17 an hour. Applicators and supervisors earn somewhat more.

Exterminators cannot be claustrophobic, as a large part of the job is climbing under homes, in attics and crawlspaces, and other tight spots.

Some pest controllers also receive commissions based on the number of jobs they contract.

The number of jobs in the pest control industry is esti-mated to grow slightly in the next decade. As homeowners grow more reluctant to resort to difficult and less effective do-it-yourself methods, demand for professional pest controllers will increase. As an increase in environmental concerns has led to the banning of some pesticides, more sophisticated forms of pest control management will be needed. This increased specialization should lead to more jobs and higher salaries.

FOR MORE INFORMATION

ORGANIZATIONS

Association of Structural Pest Control Regulatory
  Officials
663 Lacy Oak Drive
Chesapeake, VA 23220
Website: http://www.aspcro.org
This professional association is composed of the
  structural pest control regulatory officials of any
  of the fifty states that helps to promote better
  understanding of pest control laws.

National Pest Management Association
10460 North Street
Fairfax, VA 22030
(800) 678-6722
Website: https://www.npmapestworld.org
The goal of this association is to promote the
  pest controller industry through education for
  professionals and consumers.

BOOKS

Gordon, Daniel S. *From Technician to CEO: The Evolution of a High-Growth Pest Control and Lawn Care Company.* Cleveland, OH: North Coast Media, 2014.

Kramer, Richard, and Joshua Kramer. *PCT Technician's Handbook.* 4th ed. Valley View, OH: GIE Inc., 2012.

WEBSITES

Because of the changing nature of internet links, Rosen Publishing has developed an online list of websites related to the subject of this book. This site is updated regularly. Please use this link to access the list:

http://www.rosenlinks.com/CCWC/houses

CHAPTER 10

HOME APPLIANCE REPAIR PERSON

When you were younger, did you enjoy taking apart your toys (and your parents' gadgets) and putting (or trying to put) them back together again? If you still like mechanical puzzles, you might want to consider the challenge of solving them for a living—as a home appliance repairer.

WHAT THEY DO

A house is not a complete home without the basic appliances we all rely upon: refrigerators, freezers, stoves, microwaves, washers and dryers, air conditioners, and vacuum cleaners. When one of them breaks down and we suddenly find ourselves unable to cook our food or wash our clothes, we realize how important it is to have a fast, reliable, and efficient home-appliance repair person.

When a machine starts leaking or making strange noises, or stops functioning altogether, it is time to call a home appliance repairer. There is usually a difference between specialists who repair small appliances and those

Because of the size, weight, and immobility of many home appliances, it's easier for repairs to be made in the home by a trained professional.

who tackle large ones. In general, small appliance repairers are trained to fix various portable items ranging from microwaves to blenders. They usually work out of their own shops. Meanwhile, specialists in large, more mechanically complex appliances—such as refrigerators and dishwashers—tend to specialize in only one or two appliances. Because of the size of these appliances, they make house calls.

As a home appliance repairer, the first thing you'll do upon arriving at a client's home will be to check for visible clues—loose parts, leaks, odd noises, signs of rust or wear—to determine what is wrong. Aside from your knowledge of specific appliances, you'll need to consult service manuals to figure out the exact problem and how to fix it. You might have to take the appliance apart to check inner mechanisms such as wiring and electronics systems. Equipment such as voltmeters and wattmeters are used to test these systems for flaws.

Faulty parts such as gears, switches, belts, motors, and electronic circuit boards must be repaired or replaced. Before reassembling the appliance, you will need to clean, oil, and tighten all parts, leaving it in perfect operating condition. In terms of refrigerators and air conditioners, you have to exercise extreme caution due to the chemical refrigerants used to cool these appliances. Potentially dangerous to people and the environment, refrigerants have to be treated and disposed of with great care. Other potential job hazards include electrical shocks and muscle sprains from lifting heavy objects.

A repairer is nothing without his or her tool kit. This includes wrenches, pliers, and screwdrivers, as well as more specialized tools such as soldering guns and electrical equipment. In your truck or van (you can't be a large appliance repairer without a driver's license), you will usually have a stock of spare parts, too. Repairers who do house calls usually service four or five homes in a day. Aside from regular service calls, you'll have to deal with emergencies in which appliances are leaking dangerous fluids or gas is escaping. Most repairers work standard daytime hours, although some may work overtime and on weekends.

Although some repairers have their own small businesses and repair shops, most work for retailers such as home and electronic appliance stores and department stores. When a customer purchases a new appliance such as a refrigerator or washing machine, a home appliance service person is in charge of delivering the new product, installing it, and showing the owner how to operate it safely.

Home appliance repair requires good attention to detail, a sharp eye for spotting problems, and skill in working one-on-one with customers.

If you work for a large repair shop or service center, over time you may work your way up to supervisor, parts manager, or service manager. Along with technical know-how, you will need to have good interpersonal skills for these managerial positions.

CAREER PREP

In most cases, home appliance repairers require a high school diploma. As a repairer, you will need to be able to read instruction manuals (usually in English) and follow diagrams. Actual training usually takes place on the job. You usually start off by learning all there is to know about one type of appliance before mastering another. A part-time or summer job repairing appliances or any kind of mechanical or electronics equipment can provide you with good experience. Familiarity with basic electronics is increasingly important as more appliances are manufactured with electronic (as opposed to manual) control systems.

Since larger appliances are more complex, repairers of equipment such as refrigerators and washing machines often take specialized training courses at a trade school or community college. Many employers seek job candidates who have completed one- or two-year training programs at vocational high schools or community colleges. Large appliance makers, such as Whirlpool or Maytag, often have their own training programs available to their employees as well as repairers who regularly sell and service their appliances. Manufacturers frequently offer workshops and seminars to repairers to keep them up to date with new technology.

Although not necessary, your job prospects improve if you become a certified home appliance repairer. Numerous associations, such as the International Society of Certified Electronics Technicians (ISCET) and the Professional Service Association (PSA), offer certification training programs followed by exams that test your ability to detect problems and repair major home appliances. Repairing refrigerators requires you to receive EPA certification.

SALARY AND JOB OUTLOOK

In 2015, the average salary for a home appliance repairer, including commission, was $38,820 a year. Repairers who are starting out can expect to earn around $21,000, while those with a few years of experience can earn close to $60,000. Earnings vary depending on the region in which you work and the amount of skill and knowledge required to fix a certain appliance. Along with their salary, some repairers also earn commission based on the number of appliances they fix in one day.

As appliances become more technologically sophisticated—and therefore more expensive—homeowners will increasingly call upon skilled repairers instead of trading in their appliances for newer models. This will lead to more jobs working for manufacturers, dealers, and large chain stores, where supervisors can train employees to understand new features and technology. Without access to this knowledge, small repair shops and self-employed repairers will find it increasingly difficult to survive.

FOR MORE INFORMATION

ORGANIZATIONS

International Society of Certified Electronics
   Technicians (ISCET)
3000-A Landers Street
Fort Worth, TX 76107-5642
(800) 946-0201
Website: http://www.iscet.org
ISCET runs education and training programs, which
   certify technicians in the electronics and appliance
   service industry. Its website includes an online store
   and career center.

North American Retail Dealers Association
222 South Riverside Plaza, Suite 2100
Chicago, IL 60606
(800) 621-0298
Website: http://www.narda.com
This nonprofit trade association represents
   independent retailers that sell and service all types
   of consumer home products. It offers information
   about education and training programs and provides
   business services.

Professional Service Association
1526 Howard Avenue
Marengo, IA 52301
(888) 777-8851
Website: http://www.psaworld.com
This independent trade association is dedicated to
promoting the highest standards of quality service
in the appliance service industry. Our purpose
is to be the voice of the independent service
provider and to assess and identify industry-related
problems and provide solutions.

United Servicers Association
3501 N. Southport Avenue, Suite 199
Chicago, IL 60657
(800) 683-2558
Website: http://www.unitedservicers.com
This organization is run by service people dedicated
to helping professional repairers operate successful
businesses in Canada and the United States.

BOOKS

Geier, Michael. *How to Diagnose and Fix Everything Electronic*. 2nd ed. New York, NY: McGraw-Hill, 2015.
Kleinert, Eric. *Troubleshooting and Repairing Major Appliances*. New York, NY: McGraw-Hill, 2012.

WEBSITES

Because of the changing nature of internet links, Rosen Publishing has developed an online list of websites related to the subject of this book. This site is updated regularly. Please use this link to access the list:

http://www.rosenlinks.com/CCWC/houses

CHAPTER 11

LANDSCAPER

Many house owners can tell you that a home isn't complete without a well-planned garden. Even residents of condominium complexes and apartment buildings pay increasing attention to the landscaping possibilities of courtyards, terraces, driveways, and rooftops. Arranging a garden's elements—from trees, shrubs, and flowers to footpaths, decks, fences, and lighting—is the job of a landscaper. If you're creative and love nature, you might consider becoming a residential landscaper.

WHAT THEY DO

Landscape workers are involved in producing and maintaining a home's exterior spaces. Although landscapers usually don't create these spaces—planning and design is usually done by certified landscape architects with four-year specialized degrees—they are in charge of making sure exteriors stay both functional and beautiful. This involves planting, trimming, and tending to flowers, shrubs, and trees to keep them attractive and healthy. Transporting and

Landscape artists have to know a lot about plants in order to spot which ones are weeds and which ones were planted there deliberately. Some plants grow best in certain environments. A good working knowledge of plants is key to success.

spreading soil, mulch, fertilizers, and pesticides are jobs you will need to perform on a seasonal basis. Other gardening duties include seeding, fertilizing, watering, and mowing lawns. Of course, the more you know about different types of plants and flowers, their needs, and the best growing conditions, the better you will be able to look after them.

While most people think landscaping deals primarily with gardens, landscape workers often tackle a variety of projects. These could include leveling sloped land, building brick garden walls, constructing wooden fences, or laying paths of wood, tile, or ornamental stones. Installing outdoor porch lights, setting up a sprinkler system, and building a fountain, deck, or veranda are also common jobs carried out by landscapers.

As you can imagine, most of this work involves a fair amount of physical effort. Since you will be required to do a lot of lifting, climbing, digging, bending, stretching, and carrying, you will need to be in good physical shape. While many of the tools you will use arc motorized equipment such as mini-tractors, mowers, hedge trimmers, and chain saws, others will be manual tools such as shovels, rakes, hoes, hand saws, shears, and clippers. Exposure to extreme temperatures, annoying insects, and the odd thorn or splinter are also part of being a landscaper.

Although many landscapers work all year round, the types of jobs performed depend on the seasons. For example, in autumn, you'll rake and clear dead leaves and branches, while in the winter you'll need to cover plants and shovel snow. In the springtime, you'll be busy clearing debris and planting new bulbs and seeds. Climate changes mean different tasks during different times of the year depending on if you're working in southern Canada and the northern United States or in regions such as Florida, California, and Arizona, where it is warm throughout the year.

Around a quarter of all landscape workers are self-employed. They work either on their own or, depending on the size of a job, with a partner or small team of workers on a project-to-project basis. As a self-employed landscaper, you have to be good at advertising your services. As well, you'll need to be determined in terms of seeking out new projects and clients. Most landscape workers, however, prefer to work on a contract basis for large landscape firms. Over time, you can work your way up to supervisory positions. Supervisors manage workers and the financial aspects of each project—for example, the costs of materials, tools, and labor—while taking into account the client's budget. They are responsible for making sure that the final landscape project meets with the client's requirements.

CAREER PREP

No formal education is required to be a landscaper. Some vocational high schools offer courses in landscaping or gardening as do community colleges and private gardening associations. However, the simplest way to gain some initial experience as a landscaper is to work, whether paid or as a volunteer, in your own garden or that of a relative or neighbor. Many small landscaping firms contract students for seasonal help, particularly in the spring and summer. A city's department of parks also routinely hires students for summer jobs as groundskeepers as do hotels and resorts, golf courses, and botanical gardens. Such jobs will not only give you experience but important contacts as well. Specialized

Landscaping requires excellent planning skills, especially for large gardens. Some landscapers plan by hand. Others might use a landscaping app.

landscaping courses at a junior or agricultural college can prepare you for starting your own landscaping business or moving toward a career as a freelance landscape designer.

Once you have a certain amount of work experience combined with training, you can pass a written exam that will make you a certified landscaper. Various professional organizations, such as PLANET (the Professional Landscape Network), offer such certification. Although not necessary, certification gives you an edge in obtaining jobs and earning more money.

SALARY AND JOB OUTLOOK

Earnings for landscape workers are not very high. According to the US Bureau of Labor Statistics for 2015, the average American landscape worker earned $12.31 an hour. Supervisors of landscaping companies earned close to $20. Depending on how often you work and your degree of experience, you can earn between $25,000 and $63,000 a year, although managers of large firms or very successful entrepreneurs can earn more.

Opportunities for landscapers are expected to increase over the next decade. The combination of low earnings and tiring physical labor results in significant job turnover. As a result, landscaping firms are often looking for new workers. Meanwhile, most busy homeowners have full-time jobs and less time to take care of their own gardens. At the same time, they are placing increasing importance on the environment in general and on their own exteriors as spaces for relaxation and leisure. In fact, homeowners are entertaining in their yards and on their decks more than ever before. Furthermore, people selling their homes have discovered that well-kept gardens add to the value of one's property. For all of these reasons, homeowners will increasingly turn to landscapers to create and maintain their grounds and gardens.

FOR MORE INFORMATION

ORGANIZATIONS

American Nursery and Landscape Association
525 9th Street NW, Suite 800
Washington, DC 20004
(202) 789-2900
Website: https://americanhort.org
This association provides education, research, and
    public-relations services to planters, retailers,
    designers, and landscapers.

National Association of Landscape Professionals
950 Herndon Parkway, Suite 450
Herndon, VA 20170
(703) 736-9666
Website: https://www.landscapeprofessionals.org
This association promotes an exchange of business and
    technical ideas for landscapers who want to create
    and operate businesses.

BOOKS

Holmes, Roger, and Rita Buchanan. *Midwest Home
    Landscaping*. New York, NY: Creative Homeowner
    Press, 2010.

Messervy, Julie Moir. *Landscaping Ideas That Work.* Newtown, CT: Tauton Press, 2013.

Penick, Pam. *Lawn Gone! Low-Maintenance, Sustainable, Attractive Alternatives for Your Yard.* New York, NY: Ten Speed Press, 2013.

WEBSITES

Because of the changing nature of internet links, Rosen Publishing has developed an online list of websites related to the subject of this book. This site is updated regularly. Please use this link to access the list:

http://www.rosenlinks.com/CCWC/houses

CHAPTER 12

PROFESSIONAL HOME STAGER

When people prepare to sell their house or apartment, the biggest obstacle they encounter is how to stop thinking of their private living space as a home full of personal objects and cherished memories. According to real estate agents, they should be thinking of their home as a product that must attract as many buyers as possible. Because it's often hard for home-owners to do this in an objective manner, they are increasingly relying on experts, called stagers, to do it for them. If you like the idea of using your creative flair with homes to "set the stage" for prospective buyers, you might want to investigate this emerging profession.

WHAT THEY DO

The term "homestaging" was first used by an interior designer from Seattle named Barb Schwarz. In 1972, Schwarz became a real estate agent and began consulting with home-owners on how they could "stage" their properties to sell them for more money. Schwarz—who, in 2001, founded the

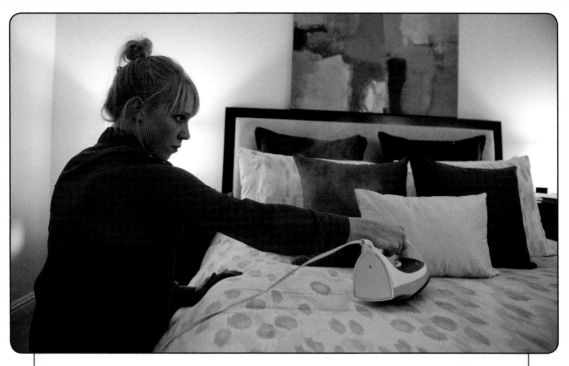

Potential homeowners react better to a fresh, organized home than a disorganized one. Home stagers work hard to give potential home buyers a pleasant experience when walking in to what might be a future home for the first time.

International Association of Home Staging Professionals—advised sellers to think of their homes as a theater stage set, with buyers as the audience and the stager as the director.

The trick to staging a home is to de-clutter, neutralize, or bland it (common terms used by stagers). In doing so, you try to remove signs of its owners. Prospective buyers can get distracted by personal mementos such as photos and might get turned off by highly personalized design choices such as brilliant purple walls, shag carpeting, enormous plants, or fluorescent lighting. When buyers view a home, they want to be able to visualize their own possessions inside it. They also need to see all of a home's features—from front doors and wooden floors to space and natural light—in their best possible light. As a stager, you'll work with sellers, helping them store or get rid of clutter, thus transforming their house or apartment into an ideal home.

As a stager—also known as a fluffer, enhancer, or styler—you'll need to have good organizational skills and a strong sense of design. You also need to have good people skills. Selling, moving, and opening up their homes to strangers is stressful for many people. They may feel defensive about having to get rid of clutter and touchy about suggestions such as hiding cat litter or taking down provocative artwork. It takes a sensitive touch to deal with many sellers and convince them to makeover their homes.

Some stagers work for real estate firms as selling agents. Others have their own freelance business, selling their services directly to homeowners. Depending on your clients' needs and budgets, you might only need to give consultations, providing tips on what sellers can do to improve their home. In other cases, you might be in charge of getting rid of and acquiring new furniture (either buying or renting); finding storage solutions;

SOME TIPS OF THE TRADE

The 50 percent rule: Clutter is often the number-one problem for stagers. Some use the 50 percent rule: storing, giving away, or selling half of people's accumulated belongings to give a home a spacious, clean look.

Neutral colors: Repainting walls in soothing neutral tones often increases the sense of space, light, and cleanliness of a home.

Décor: Most people have too much furniture, hence some needs to be stored or given away. In the event furniture is old, worn, or mismatched, stagers can buy or even rent furniture.

Extreme cleaning: Everything (including curtains and carpets) needs to be professionally and thoroughly cleaned. This gives buyers a sense that the entire house is in tip-top condition.

Ambiance: Many stagers recommend playing low, soothing music such as jazz and having fresh-cut flowers and welcoming smells, such as scented candles or home-baked cookies.

Props: Accents such as throw pillows, fancy bedding, or extra fluffy towels in the bathroom are important details.

Storage: Empty closets and cupboards. Store or get rid of clothes in a clothes closet to make the closet appear more spacious. Organize clothes according to color and hang on wooden hangers.

cleaning, painting, and redecorating; and even suggesting renovations. If your client owns a house, you'll need to focus on the exterior as well, along with the garage, driveway, yards, surrounding trees, and shrubbery. For this reason, you'll need to cultivate good working relationships with retailers (of furniture and construction supplies), painters, movers, landscapers, and other related tradespeople. Although a radical makeover can be costly— some sellers can spend between $5,000 and $15,000 on staging—experts estimate that for every $1 spent, a home's value increases by $1.50. Many sellers are so happy with the transformation stagers perform that they hire them to help decorate when they move into their new homes.

CAREER PREP

There is no specific education recommended if you want to become a stager. Taking courses or seminars in interior design and real estate sales can be useful. It is also a good idea to read decorating magazines, books, or websites and to watch TV programs such as *Trading Spaces*. The International Association of Home Staging Professionals runs training programs and workshops with classroom and hands-on courses that give participants a certificate in professional staging.

Attention to detail is important in home staging. A single burned out lightbulb might change the mood of an entire room.

SALARY AND JOB OUTLOOK

Most stagers will work with a homeowner for a day or two. Fees vary depending on the market you are in. However, on average, stagers charge between $60 and $85 an hour as a basic consulting fee. Depending on the number of rooms involved, you can earn between $700 and $3,000 per project. For major overhauls, you can earn much more. For example, one home stager who arranged for painting and the removal of columns, rearranged furniture, improved the lighting, and brought in accessories such as plants and throw pillows for a two-bedroom Manhattan apartment charged a fee of $1,600.

Popular on the West Coast for over a decade, staging is a new but rapidly growing field, particularly in large urban centers such as New York and Toronto. As real estate markets continue to grow and more agents and sellers are recognizing the value of a staged home, there should be increasing opportunity for those who are interested in this field.

FOR MORE INFORMATION

ORGANIZATIONS

International Association of Home Staging Professionals
4807 Clayton Road, Suite 100
Concord, CA 94521
(800) 392-7161
Website: http://stagedhomes.com
   This association offers information and training
   programs for those who want to become professional
   stagers. Its website provides a list of professional
   stagers and the homes they have staged that are
   for sale.

International Interior Design Association (IIDA)
222 Merchandise Mart, Suite 567
Chicago, IL 60654
(888) 799-4432
Website: https://www.iida.org
The International Interior Design Association was
   created to maintain professional standards in the field
   of twenty-four-hour decorating. IIDA offers training
   and certification.

BOOKS

Smithers, Dana J. *Start & Run a Home Staging Business.* Vancouver, BC, Canada: Self-Counsel Press, 2011.
Toth, Tori. *Feel at Home: Home Staging Secrets for a Quick and Easy Sell.* Hampton, VA: Morgan James Publishing, 2015.

WEBSITES

Because of the changing nature of internet links, Rosen Publishing has developed an online list of websites related to the subject of this book. This site is updated regularly. Please use this link to access the list:

http://www.rosenlinks.com/CCWC/houses

GLOSSARY

APPRENTICE Someone who learns the basics of a job by working under the supervision of a professional.

ASBESTOS A mineral used for fireproofing, for insulation, and as a building material that, if inhaled over long periods of time, can cause cancer.

BLAND Tranquil, inoffensive, lacking in distinct flavor.

BROKER Someone who acts as an agent for others, as in negotiating contracts, purchases, or sales, in return for a fee or commission.

CONTRACTOR Someone who agrees to furnish materials or perform services for a given price.

ERGONOMICS The science of using information about human beings to design spaces suitable for their needs.

FLUCTUATE To rise and fall.

FUMIGATION Using smoke or fumes to get rid of pests.

LIABILITY An obligation, responsibility, or debt.

MENTOR A wise or trusted counselor or teacher.

MULCH A protective covering, usually of leaves, straw, or peat, placed around plants to prevent the evaporation of moisture, the freezing of roots, and the growth of weeds.

NEUTRAL A color—such as gray, black, or white—that lacks hue.

PARQUET A patterned wood surface (often used for floors).

PORTFOLIO A portable case for holding material, such as photographs or drawings, as well as the representative work a person keeps in it.

RADON A colorless, radioactive, inert gaseous element formed by the radioactive decay of radium.

REFRIGERANT A substance—such as air, ammonia, water, or carbon dioxide—used to provide cooling.

SCAFFOLDING A temporary platform, supported from below or suspended from above, on which workers sit or stand when performing tasks at heights above the ground.

SCALE Proportion, as it relates to a space.

SEEPAGE The process of water seeping or oozing.

SOLDERING A means of joining or cementing two metallic parts together with melted tin or lead.

STUCCO A fine plaster used in decoration and ornamentation of walls.

UNETHICAL Dishonorable, immoral.

VOLTMETER An instrument used to measure, in volts, the differences of potential between different points of an electrical circuit.

WATTMETER An instrument used to measure electric power, in watts.

BIBLIOGRAPHY

Gillman, Steve. "House Painting 101: How to Get Started as a Part-Time Painter." *The Penny Hoarder*. August 13, 2014. http://www.thepennyhoarder.com/house -painting.

Goulet, Tag. "10 Steps to an Interior Decorator Career." IAP Career College. March 15, 2016. https://www .iapcollege.com/interior-decorator-career.

Kaplan Real Estate Education. "Is a Career in Real Estate Right for You?" November 12, 2015. https://www .kapre.com/resources/real-estate/is-a-career-in-real -estate-right-for-you.

Little, Shelley. "10 Things You Should Know About Becoming an Interior Designer." Freshome. October 13, 2014. http://freshome.com/2014/10/13/10-things -you-should-know-about-becoming-an-interior -designer.

Lupo, Lisa Jo. "Get a Job! In Pest Control." About Home. September 1, 2016. http://pestcontrol.about.com/od /callingapestcontrolco/a/So-You-Want-A-Job-In-Pest -Control.htm.

INDEX

ABOUT THE AUTHOR

Rebecca Pelos is a nonfiction writer with experience in job hunting and career guidance. She lives in Tennessee.

Alice Beco is a writer who specializes in nonfiction topics.

PHOTO CREDITS

Cover, p. 1 Hurse Photo/Shutterstock.com; pp. 4–5, 13, 78–79, 86–87 wavebreakmedia/Shutterstock.com; pp. 8, 10 Rawpixel.com/Shutterstock.com; pp. 17, 64–65 Kzenon/Shutterstock.com; p. 19 ullstein bild/Getty Images; p. 26 bikeriderlondon/Shutterstock.com; p. 28 Oleg Vinnichenko/Shutterstock .com; p. 31 Syda Productions/Shutterstock.com; p. 35 MyLoupe/Universal Images Group/Getty Images; p. 36 Chicago Tribune/Tribune News Service/ Getty Images; pp. 39, 115 Bloomberg/Getty Images; pp. 44–45 Africa Studio/Shutterstock.com; p. 47 VGstockstudio/Shutterstock.com; pp. 54–55 luanateutzi/Shutterstock.com; p. 60 Elena Elisseeva/Shutterstock.com; p. 67 © iStockphoto.com/Pamela Moore; p. 70 Diego Cervo/Shutterstock.com; pp. 76–77 Andy Dean Photography/Shutterstock.com; p. 92 The Sydney Morning Herald/Fairfax Media/Getty Images; p. 97 Andrey_Popov/Shutterstock .com; p. 99 Photographee.eu/Shutterstock.com; p. 107 JP Wallet/Shutterstock .com; p. 110 Toa55/Shutterstock.com; p. 119 © iStockphoto.com/Jodi Jacobson; cover and interior design elements © iStockphoto.com/David Shultz (dots), Melamory/Shutterstock.com (hexagon pattern), Lost & Taken (boxed text background texture), VoodooDot/Shutterstock.com (chapter opener pages icons).

Designer: Brian Garvey; Editor and Photo Researcher: Bethany Bryan

O Christmas Tree

By Debbie Trafton O'Neal
Illustrated by Ande Cook

Augsburg Books
Bringing Families Together
for Children & Families

As the evergreen tree remains green
throughout the year,
may it always remind you of God's
never-changing love for you!

O CHRISTMAS TREE

Large-quantity purchases or custom editions of this book are available at a discount from the publisher. For more information, contact the sales department at Augsburg Fortress, Publishers, 1-800-328-4648, or write to: Sales Director, Augsburg Fortress, Publishers, P.O. Box 1209, Minneapolis, MN 55440-1209.

ISBN 0-8066-4560-1

The paper used in this publication meets the minimum requirements of American National Standard for Information Sciences—Permanence of Paper for Printed Library Materials, ANSI Z329.48-1984.

Manufactured in Singapore

07   06   05   04   03   1   2   3   4   5   6   7   8   9   10

O Christmas tree, O Christmas tree,
Your branches never changing.
O Christmas tree, O Christmas tree,
Your branches never changing.

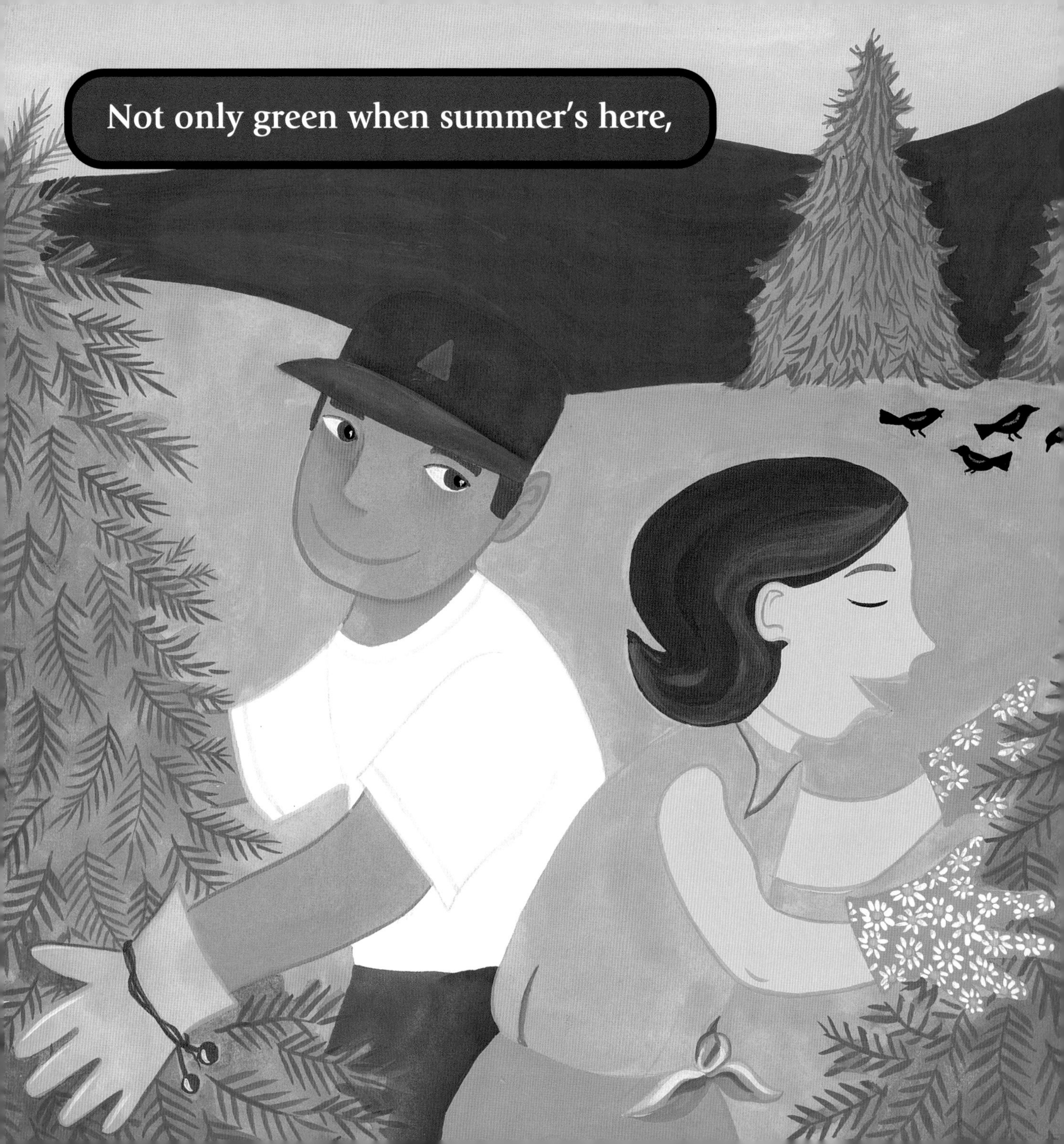
Not only green when summer's here,

But also when it's cold and drear.

O Christmas tree, O Christmas tree,
Your branches never changing.

O Christmas tree, O Christmas tree,
How lovely are your branches!

O Christmas tree, O Christmas tree,
How lovely are your branches!

The sight of you
At Christmastide

Spreads hope and gladness
Far and wide.

O Christmas tree, O Christmas tree,
How lovely are your branches!

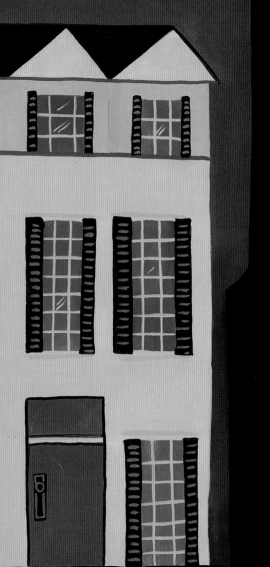

O Christmas tree, O Christmas tree,
Your lights shine out so brightly!

O Christmas tree, O Christmas tree,
Your lights shine out so brightly!

Remind me of God's love for me.

O Christmas tree, O Christmas tree,
Your lights shine out so brightly!

Christmas Family Fun

Trim the tree

Once you have your Christmas tree, the fun really begins! Decorating it can be the best part of all. Here are a few ornaments to make for your tree.

❄ Garlands wrap around your tree and can be made of almost anything you like. You can string popcorn or alternate popcorn kernels with cranberries for a touch of color. You also can string candies, small pinecones or nuts, or even pasta to make a garland!

❄ Origami ornaments: Make folded paper ornaments to decorate your tree. Find a book about origami for a few good ideas.

❄ Family photos: Frame small pictures of your friends and family and hang them on your Christmas tree.

❄ Theme trees: You might even want to give your tree a "theme"—like birds, flowers, hobbies, or collections.

Handprint tree skirt

Make a special fabric "skirt" to wrap around the base of your tree. Cut a large piece of plain, colored fabric into a circle, or use a circular tablecloth. Cut a hole about the size of your Christmas tree trunk into the center, then cut a slit from one outer edge to the center hole. Let family members paint their hands with silver or gold acrylic paint and make handprints on the skirt. Then wrap the fabric around the base of the tree.

Save room to add prints in the years to come. If you add handprints to this tree skirt every year, you will be saving a precious part of your growing-up years.

Paper chains

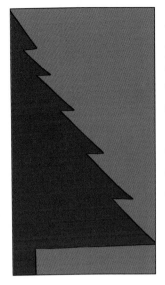

Many people make paper chains to hang as garlands on their tree, to help them count the days until Christmas arrives, or to decorate other parts of their house. Copy this drawing onto colorful paper and follow these directions to make tree-shaped paper chains.

Cut or tape together a strip of paper as long as you want your chain to be. Trace the half tree shape onto one end of the paper strip, then fold the paper back and forth, accordion style, until the entire piece is folded. Using the traced pattern, cut the tree shape into the folded paper. Then unfold and hang your paper chain.

Pipe cleaner stars

A legend says that Martin Luther saw stars twinkling through branches of a small fir tree as he walked home one snowy evening. The sight was so lovely that Luther took the tree home and added candles to its branches so his family could enjoy the beauty. It was the first lighted Christmas tree!

Make these pipe cleaner stars to decorate your tree and remind you of the stars that twinkled through that first Christmas tree's branches.

You can purchase shiny metallic chenille stems at a craft store. To make stars that look like snowflakes, cut two chenille stems in half and twist them together in the center. Add other half stems, twisting them onto the original pieces. You can add as many pieces as you like. Attach a ribbon or cord for hanging, or just set the twinkling stars in the branches of your Christmas tree.

Colored fire cones

If you have a fireplace, you will enjoy making and using these colored fire cones.

In a bowl, mix white glue and water to about the consistency of paint. Use a thick paintbrush to coat pinecones with the mixture, then roll the cones in a bowl filled with fire-color crystals (from the fireplace equipment section of a local hardware store). Let the crystal-covered cones dry on an inverted egg carton, then keep these in a basket by your fireplace. Toss a few cones into the fire whenever your family is gathered to enjoy the holiday season this year. (These make great gifts, too!)

Christmas dream pillows

People throughout the ages have made special "dream pillows"—pouches filled with fragrant herbs and flowers to tuck under their pillows for a night of sweet dreams. You can make a dream pillow to help keep the Christmas season in your house all year long.

When you take down your real Christmas tree, fill a bowl with dried evergreen needles. (If they aren't dry yet, slide fresh needles off the tree into a bowl; then stir them every day, and they will dry naturally.)

Sew Christmas cotton fabric or muslin into a small bag, leaving a small opening to insert the needles. (A funnel makes the task less messy.)

Don't fill the bag too full; it should be loosely packed. Sew the opening closed, then slip the dream pillow under your sleeping pillow or behind a cushion on your favorite chair. Every time the pillow is moved, it will release the scent of your Christmas tree.

O Christmas Tree

O Christmas tree, O Christmas tree,
Your branches never changing.

Not only green when summer's here,
But also when it's cold and drear.

O Christmas tree, O Christmas tree,
Your branches never changing.

O Christmas tree, O Christmas tree,
How lovely are your branches!

The sight of you at Christmastide
Spreads hope and gladness far and wide.

O Christmas tree, O Christmas tree,
How lovely are your branches!

O Christmas tree, O Christmas tree,
Your lights shine out so brightly!

The gifts beneath you that I see
Remind me of God's love for me.

O Christmas tree, O Christmas tree,
Your lights shine out so brightly!

O Christmas Tree (O Tannenbaum)

1 O Christ - mas tree, O Christ-mas tree, your bran - ches ne - ver
2 O Christ - mas tree, O Christ-mas tree, how love - ly are your
3 O Christ - mas tree, O Christ-mas tree, your lights shine out so

chang - ing. Not on - ly green when sum - mer's here, but
bran - ches! The sight of you at Christ - mas - tide spreads
bright - ly! The gifts be - neath you that I see re -

al - so when it's cold and drear. O Christ - mas tree, O
hope and glad - ness far and wide. O Christ - mas tree, O
mind me of God's love for me. O Christ - mas tree, O

Christ-mas tree, your bran - ches ne - ver chang - ing.
Christ-mas tree, how love - ly are your bran - ches!
Christ-mas tree, your lights shine out so bright - ly!

Text: traditional; revised text st. 2 copyright © 2001 Augsburg Fortress; st. 3 Debbie Trafton O'Neal
Music: German folk song